IN & AROUND EASINGWOLD

The Passage Of Time

Paul Chrystal

G H Smith & Son

Introduction

This is the first book to be published which provides a history of Easingwold in pictures and in words: the 250 black and white, sepia and colour photographs provide a fascinating insight into life in Easingwold and the surrounding villages at the turn of the 20th century and in the earlier years of that century. In so doing it takes the reader on an intriguing journey through the past, which includes Crayke, Ampleforth, Coxwold, Byland, Wass, Kilburn, Husthwaite, Brafferton, Helperby, Sheriff Hutton, Sutton-on-the Forest, Tollerton, Raskelf and Myton-on-Swale.

In Easingwold we hear the history of the Market Place and town hall, St Joseph's Convent, Claypenny Colony for 'mental defectives', St Monica's Hospital and the various schools and places of religion down the years. We meet John Wesley, General Booth, Baden-Powell and Bear Grylls on their visits here and colourful residents like Billy Sweep reformed alcoholic, Nana Ran Dan licensee, Peggy Johnson cucking stool victim, and Katherine Love, benefactor. We trace the history of various clubs and societies here: the Scouts, Easingwold Singers, the Rifle Club, the Town Band and Easingwold Angels Ladies Football Club, and of long standing businesses like Clarks, Dooleys and Reynards. Easingwold's Light Railway and its long tradition of printing and publishing – from Thomas Gill to GH Smith - are covered, as are the surviving public houses in Market Place and Long Street and the town's involvement in the Boer War and the two world wars.

Moving out of town we arrive first at Ampleforth to learn the fascinating histories of the College and Abbey; the battle and Abbey at Byland are covered next before moving on to Coxwold with its association with Laurence Sterne and the Cromwells. Crayke is next with its castle, hall and two witches and then Brafferton and Helperby for the Gallant Band of Five. On to Kilburn with its famous White Horse and even more famous Mouseman, and then on to Myton – known for its connections with Saracen slaying, the White Battle and the von Bismarks. We move on to Raskelf to learn about the almost unique wooden tower there and the pinfold, Sherriff Hutton with its two castles and Sutton for more associations with Tristram Shandy and Dr Slop. Tollerton Ladies Cricket comes next before arriving in Wass to see the past and present there characterised by Victorian philanthropy and 21st century hospitality in the Wombwell Arms. Finally, it is to Husthwaite with William Peckitt – one of England's finest glass painters.

Altogether a captivating journey around Easingwold and its neighbouring villages which will fascinate and delight with its 250 photographs, documents and their accompanying descriptions.

Paul Chrystal, York June 2012

First Published 2012

Published by G H Smith & Son
Market Place
Easingwold
York
YO61 3AB

www.ghsmith.com

Copyright © Paul Chrystal 2012

ISBN 978-0-904775-62-4

Acknowledgements

Special thanks go to Rupert Smith at GH Smith, Easingwold who supplied many of the old photographs and images from the Easingwold Advertiser. Thanks too go to Deborah Selkirk at Easingwold School for use of school pictures and for access to their archive; to Jane Wintermeyer, Chairman of The Easingwold Singers; Edward Kendall, Honorary Secretary, Easingwold Rifle Club; Helen Kirk, Forest of Galtres Society; Nick Clark, Clark the Bakers; Kira Robinson, Mark Sherwood and Katie Wilkinson of Easingwold Angels Ladies FC; Chris Pearson of the Laurence Sterne Trust for permission to use the cartoon on page 87; John Lister, Easingwold Players; Ian Walker, The Wombwell Arms; David Bottomley, for permission to use images published in his Brafferton & Helperby: A Millenium History; and to my good friend Peter Lawson for translating the Bismark post card. Peter Bousfield generously and patiently provided the pictures of Myton – along with much invaluable information. Fr Kentigern Hagan, Warden of the Visitor Centre at Ampleforth Abbey, kindly showed me round. The modern photography is by the author unless stated otherwise.

About the Author

Paul Chrystal is author of the following titles in the Amberley Publishing Through Time series published in 2010 and 2011: Knaresborough; North York Moors (which includes Kilburn and Coxwold); Tadcaster; Villages Around York; Richmond & Swaledale; Northallerton; Hartlepool; In & Around York; Harrogate; York Places of Learning; Redcar, Marske & Saltburn; Vale of York (which includes chapters on Easingwold and Thirsk and the surrounding area). And in 2012: York Trade & Industry; In & Around Pocklington; Barnard Castle & Teesdale; Lifestations of the North East; Industrial Model Villages; Coffee, Tea & Cocoa; Cadbury & Fry; Confectionery in Yorkshire; Scarborough –A Second Collection; Selby and Goole.

Other books by Paul Chrystal: A Children's History of Harrogate & Knaresborough, 2011; A to Z of Knaresborough History Revised Edn, 2011; A to Z of York History, 2012; Chocolate: The British Chocolate Industry, Shire 2011; History of Chocolate in York, Pen & Sword 2012; The Rowntree Family, Amberley 2012; Women in Ancient Rome, Amberley 2012.

As well as being author and historian, Paul was a medical publisher for thirty years and, more recently, a bookseller; he lives near York.

Easingwold Inns: in the 1820s Easingwold could boast twelve public houses later rising to twenty-eight, ten of which were in Long Street and four in Market Place; in the 1930s there were still nineteen around town.

CHAPTER ONE: EASINGWOLD

OPENING CEREMONY by Col. LEGARD —
of the MINIATURE RIFLE RANGE EASINGWOLD. AUG 23.1906.

The Miniature Rifle Range

The old photograph shows Colonel Legard inspecting a detachment of the Yorkshire Regiment Volunteers on the occasion of the opening of the Miniature Rifle Range in the Town Hall on August 23rd 1906. The medals on the soldiers in the centre and on the one behind are South African campaign medals. The George Hotel is visible in the background. The town's 1921 granite obelisk war memorial commemorates fifty-seven fallen from World War I and fifteen from World War II; their names also can be seen on a plaque in the parish church. See also page 36.

Church Lane

Church Lane features in the old picture. The parish church is St John the Baptist and All Saints on Church Hill and is largely 14th century although Doomsday mentions an earlier church and a priest in the town. The lych gate was originally at Huntington parish church, north of York. St John was but one of five Easingwold places of religion by 1840: the others were a Wesleyan Methodist Chapel from 1886 which replaced the 1816 Chapel; the Independents' chapel built in 1820; the Primitive Methodists' chapel from 1840 and St John the Evangelist Roman Catholic Church completed in the 1830s. It was designed in 1830 by the architect, Charles Hansom, the brother of York's Joseph Hansom – inventor of the 'Hansom cab'.

'Twelve carucates of land to the geld'

The west side of Market Place showing H Shaw, the veterinary surgeon's in the 1930s. From Domesday we learn that in 1086: 'In Easingwold are 12 carucates of land to the geld, which 7 ploughs could plough. Morcar held these as 1 manor tre. Now it is in the king's hand, and there are 10 villans having 4 ploughs. [There is] a church with a priest… woodland pasture 2 leagues long and 2 broad. All together 3 leagues long and 2 broad. Then worth 32l ; now 20s.' The devaluation was caused by the William's scorched earth campaign that was the punitive Harrying of the North.

'God with Us'

This once half-timbered house in Spring Street was rebuilt in 1907 and still bears the inscription 'God with us, 1664' - 'God with us' being a Parliamentarian rallying cry at Marston Moor. Another stood next to the Catholic Church in Long Street. The timber-framed thatched house at the cross roads in Uppleby with its close studding and diagonal braces at the first floor level has survived (see page 54).

The Town Hall

Pictured here in 1869 before the clock which came later in the year. The Town Hall first opened its doors on March 31st 1864; it cost £1,423 and became the venue for the county court and petty sessions. The Bulmer West Highway Board met there to oversee road and street construction; in 1872 the chairman was one John Coates of Peep o' Day and it was he who oversaw much work on the roads to and from Oswaldkirk, Stillington and Sutton-on-the-Forest. Peep o' Day was the name of a farm house near Husthwaite.

A Palfrey for a King

Agricultural machines for sale at the market, with the Angel in the background, first licensed in 1797. In 1221, Easingwold paid the King one palfrey, a small horse, for the right to hold a Saturday market every Saturday. Charles I granted a charter to George Hall in 1638 by Letters Patent from which a free market could be held every Friday, with a cattle market every other Friday from St. Matthew's Day to St. Thomas's Day, along with two fairs each year (July 6th and September 26th). In return, Hall was obliged to build and maintain the tollbooth and maintain the surrounding pavements. Economy was obviously a concern as the resulting tollbooth to the rear of the Town Hall measured a modest ten feet by six with a flight of stone steps. Before the Town Hall was built the Market Place comprised a row of houses on the north side and a double row of shambles: High and Low Shambles were in the centre of the market place where butchers traded in meat, butter and bacon along with other goods.

The Town Hall Clock

More market activity in 1903. The clock in the clock tower ticked away for 132 years and then stopped, never to go again. In its time the Town Hall has been home to the fire station, a cinema, a dance hall and is now GH Smith, printers and publishers.

Low Street

Long Street was originally called Low Street because it was the southern end of what could well be described as two towns – Uppleby being the northern, Danish settlement under the control of the Danish chief Uplleby. Low Street was inhabited by the Angles. The name Easingwold probably derives from ease which means 'rich irrigated land prone to flooding', and wold or 'forest'. Alternatively, it may come from the Saxon family name Esa.

Claypenny Hospital and the Poor House

Founded in 1932 as the Claypenny Colony for 'mental defectives' the hospital was developed on the site of the redundant Easingwold Poor Law Institution, the town's workhouse, which dated from the 1830s. Patient numbers increased from ninety in 1937 to 188 in 1938 and reached a peak of around 360 in the mid 1950s; the hospital was always notiorous for overcrowding. The numbered and lettered wards were renamed with tree names in the '50s – as reflected today in the modern apartments that make up Cedar Place – to make the place more 'humane'. There was a road house for casual vagrants, annexed to the front of the workhouse. Some of the rules of the Easingwold Poor Law Institution are interesting: no ale or spirits except by order of the surgeon; men and women to sit separately; no smoking at meals; children to be separated from parents; no smoking after 7.00pm; menus included boiled beasts heads with potatoes for dinner on Fridays and beasts or sheep's hearts roasted with potatoes on Saturday.

General Booth Arrives

General Booth visited in July 1908 and Hilda Sturge presented the bouquet. The modern picture, published in the Easingwold Advertiser, was taken during the 2012 Week of Prayer for Christian Unity.

The Galtres Centre

The Galtres Community Centre was originally a private house designed by W H Brierley, York architect. Built in 1897 for Francis Robinson, a solicitor who practiced in 'The White House' off the market place, Cpt Hugh Holdsworth of Halifax bought it in 1930. In the 1950s it fell into disuse but in 1983 reopened as the thriving community centre it is today. The Blue Bell in Uppleby was one of the town's first inns, possibly named after the fact that it would have been frequented by Scottish drovers. It was run by Anne Harrison (d. 1745), also known as Nanna Ran Dan about whom Thomas Salvin Snr who resided at the mediaeval Old Hall wrote the following tribute: 'chaste but not prude/and tho' free yet no harlot/…her extensive Charity made her esteemed./Her tongue and her hands were ungovernable/…weigh her virtues be charitable and speak well of her'.

Easingwold Green 1903

As well as the Toll Booth and the Shambles there was also a cucking stool in the Market Place which claimed its last victim, Peggy Johnson, in 1763; a row of cottages called the Squad; the town lock-up and pinfold and the inevitable stocks and a whipping post. The Butter Cross is a reconstruction of an original; a bear-baiting ring was at the north end of where the Town Hall is now.

Easingwold Post Office

The Post Office and its staff of twelve, including seven postmen, in the 1920s. In 1809 Langdale in his Topographical Dictionary of Yorkshire tells us that the Post Boy in Long Street was one of the main inns in the town; this became the New Inn, Post & Excise Office Inn pictured on the next page. In 1823 the post house was at the Fleece Inn in Long Street (see page 62). Around 1871 the Post Office moved to Market Place, sharing the building with the Yorkshire Banking Company (see page 49). In 1899 Sidney Smith, the postmaster, won the contract to carry the mail between Easingwold and Huby, a duty he performed in some style: his six horse power came in the form of a Benz motor car.

Trevelyan Temperance Hotel

The hotel in Long Street was run by a Hubert Baines, strict Methodist; he succeeded George Haynes whose name is still visible on the window in this old photo. Most likely it was named after Sir Walter Calverley Trevelyan (1797-1879) president of the UK Temperance Alliance - there are other Trevelyan hotels in Leeds and Halifax. The chimney of the Union Steam Flour Mill is visible in the distance; the mill opened in 1856, the same year as the decision to adopt the Lighting and Watching Act of William IV to enable gas lighting for the town; this led to the the Easingwold Gas and Coke Company and its gas works in Long Street in 1857. The Union Mill was probably responsible for the demise of the tower windmill on Mill Street which may have been used both as a corn mill and a mustard mill at one time or another.

Spring Street and Easingwold Spa

Other Easingwold industries in the mid nineteenth century included an iron foundry, brewing , rope walks, a tannery, and brick making and bacon and butter trade. On the retail side White's 1867 Directory tells us that there were four booksellers, five grocers, seven milliners, seven drapers, thirteen shoe and bootmakers, seventeen public houses, three marine stores and four watchmakers; also Chapman Medd & Sons cabinet makers, antique dealers and undertakers. Spring Street is named after the spring which rises half way up the street. Page tells us (History of the County of York & North Riding Vol2) that 'the best known of the chalybeate springs …are Spring Head Well and a medicinal spring in a field near the fish-pond said to resemble the Cheltenham waters. Spa Well, which is chalybeate and sulphurous, is about half a mile to the west of the town'.

Easingwold Cottage Hospital

The hospital was established in 1893 by Katherine Love, a local benefactor from a wealthy Durham mining family. Initially it was called Easingwold Cottage Hospital but was later renamed St Monica's after the mother of St Augustus. The NHS took it over in 1948; it now serves as a Community Hospital. Katherine Love was founder of the Easingwold Singers in 1903 (then called The Easingwold and District Musical Society); she was also the first Chairman of Easingwold Scouts in 1921. Mr Love was founding President of the Temperance Band in 1893.

Chapel Street 1903

The farmland on the edge of town was divided into four fields; Crayke Field to the east, Mill Field to the north where there stood a wind mill; Church Field to the north-west and Stone Field to the south. The surrounding royal Forest of Galtres had been acquired soon after the Conquest for the Norman kings: in 1316 it comprised sixty or so villages in 100,000 acres. It was at its greatest extent around 1180 extending south to the walls of York and over to Sheriff Hutton. It was gradually deforested and turned into farmland from the 17th century after the Act of Dis-Afforestation of 1629 put an end to the Forest and the Crown sold off estates held on lease. The pictures show Chapel Street in 1903 and 109 years later.

Dooley's

Dooley's is one of the few surviving shops here from the earlier part of the last century. It was established in 1937 by Mr & Mrs W Dooley whose aim it was to provide only the freshest and finest quality produce – a mission which still endures seventy-five years later. From the beginning, Dooley's sourced most of their produce from Hull Fruit market and local growers. This locally sourced produce is complemented with fruit and vegetables from the Rungis Market in Paris and from various sources in Italy and Holland.

A Windy Day in Long Street

The register of burials for any town usually makes interesting, if uncomfortable, reading, and Easingwold's for 1777-1780 is no exception: sixteen children died of smallpox, twenty-one, mainly adults, of consumption, four (children) of whooping cough, four from dropsy (heart failure); one in childbirth; two from mortification of the bowels and one each from apoplexy (stroke), palsy (paralysis), marasmus (malnutrition), gravel (kidney stones), bladder inflammation and asthma.

Clarks The Bakers

Clarks the Bakers was established around 1925 in a 17th century house at the Stillington end of Long Street by Lucy Clark who started out baking scones which she sold through the window of her house to the tarmac men from Middlesbrough and Stockton who came to build and repair the local roads. Popularity led to Lucy opening a café and so was born Clarks the Bakers. The house was later converted to become a bakery, shop and a café. The aerial view of Long Street shows a very unusual one up one down in the centre, and the stone 'pavements'.

Crawford House

The new photograph shows the splendid restored fanlight in the Grade II listed early nineteenth century Crawford House. It was the home of Thomas Crawford; next door were his heavy horse stables. Crawford was one of two businessmen offering carrier services from Easingwold to York from around the 1780s; he had a 'depot' at the Black Bull in York's Thursday Market, now St Sampson's Square, for the York-Edinburgh run. He also connected with the London wagon for collection and delivery. The old picture from 1905 shows a parade of children outside the now demolished timber framed cottage that was Shepherd's Garth in Long Street near the site of the Roman Catholic church.

The Mill

This fascinating photograph shows workmen taking a break while clearing out the pond behind the mill in Long Street in 1903 to make way for the swimming pool. From the early 1900s there was a row of four almhouses on the corner of Chapel Street and Long Street; the October 21st edition of the Easingwold Advertiser tells us that a horse had fled into one of them and tried to run up the stairs. They, like the widows' cottages in Little Lane have long been demolished. The occasion of Victoria's Diamond Jubilee in 1897 was marked by the building of four almshouses in Spring Street. The new picture depicts the Memorial Park opened in 1954 on land acquired by the Easingwold Peace Celebrations Fund and commemorates the casualties of wars after 1945.

York & Ainsty Hunt 1884

Pictured here in the Market Place, the Hunt was formed in 1816 and hunted four days a week until 1906. Perhaps its most tragic chapter was the Newby Ferry disaster of February 1869 during a meet at South Stainley. A fox swam across the flooded River Ure pursued by hounds: attempts to stop the chase were in vain so the Master and Huntsman, Sir Charles Slingsby of Scriven along with twelve others commandeered the small ferry boat - a boat which could only safely take four horses. The overloaded ferry sank, drowning Slingsby and five others. In 1929 The York and Ainsty divided into its present North and South packs. The old photograph shows the old Vicarage on the right, demolished to make way for the Galtres. The shop is FE Rookledge, chemists and booksellers, famous for his promotion of Dr Tibbles' VI-Cocoa - extremely efficacious because 'by nourishing the body the cheeks become rosy and plump, whilst the strength and nervous energy thus gained are the natural outcome of increased vitality'.

St Joseph's Convent

This mid to late 18th century house was formerly St Joseph's Convent, and previously an inn, the Rose & Crown. Its tiers of Venetian windows at each end of the building are particularly impressive. The Rose & Crown became a girls' boarding school in 1905 under the auspices of the Sisters of Mercy, taking the name of St Joseph's Convent; today it goes by the name of the Old Coach Yard. The Convent was not the first educational establishment here. In 1893 Mr FW Long was headmaster of the Westerman Grammar School for Boys which was then housed in the old New Rose & Crown building, called Longley House: head, street and building all answered to 'long'.

The Commercial

The Commercial Inn is on the site of the old Unicorn. The Unicorn here (there was another on Long Street) is but one of thirteen hostelries referred to in a broadsheet entitled A Peep at the Publicans of Easingwold and performed in the 1820s by a Mr Smith at the Theatre. The Green Tree is another and described as the place 'where the Scotchman may meet with his clan' – drovers no doubt.

The Primitive Methodist Chapel

The new picture shows the chapel which dates from 1975 and is the third on the site. The older photograph is of the first chapel. A school was added in 1860 financed by voluntary contribution, school fees and an examination grant. John Wesley probably preached at John Skaife's house on May 8th 1786 (see page 44), spending the night at a farm on the road to Stillington, and later under an apple tree in Uppleby. The shop on the right here is L.T. Storr's 'practical tailors, stationers and postcard sellers', now a private house.

Temporary Insanity in Long Street

Building work in the town today and a century ago. Long Street was nothing if not short of inns and taverns. They included, at one time or another, The Unicorn, The New Inn, The Horse Shoe, The Green Tree, New Rose & Crown, Old Rose & Crown (now Nos 83-87), The Sun and The Punch Bowl (now No 41); The Royal Oak, The Bay Horse and The Fleece at the Thirsk end which survive only as the names on the houses which replaced them (see page 62). Alcohol and Long Street sometimes did not mix, it seems: Tom Cowling died from excessive drinking at the Royal Oak in 1825 and William White, a joiner, suffered the same fate when he carelessly downed a pint of rum instead of ale in The Unicorn. Thomas Gill tells us that at The New Rose & Crown Frank Sellars 'writhing under the anguish of disappointed love in his ardent attachment to Miss Fanny Thorpe, a pretty dressmaker in the town, hung himself in the coach house' (Gill's Family Almanack, 1872.) In 1838 a lovelorn Mary Scaife from Ripon hanged herself in the kitchen of The New Inn; a verdict of Temporary Insanity was returned.

Punch & Judy

A very popular Punch & Judy show in Long Street in 1908 – although it has to be said that the photographer seems to have stolen the show, and the dog looks less than pleased. If Punch & Judy are symbolic of earlier, more violent forms of public entertainment then go no further than the Market Place. Apart from the ducking stool sited here there was the bull ring for bull baiting: in 1611 a bull reputedly (according to Gill's Family Almanack) broke its chains and gored a man and two women to death. A varied programme of entertainment at the Galtres Centre can be seen in the new picture from a January 2012 edition of the Easingwold Advertiser.

The York Hotel and Easingwold Town Band 1903

The band and members of the Easingwold branch of the United Order of Druids outside The York. First licensed in the 1840s The York was originally called The Talbot. The shop in between The York and The George was Bannisters, family grocers, hay and forage suppliers, agricultural seeds and cakes and wines and spirits; Simpson's Boot and Shoe Depot was next to The George with a branch of the York Union Bank Ltd next to that.

Easingwold Town Band 1905

Outside the Galtres. The band in Easingwold has been playing for over 100 years and is still going strong. Their website tells us: 'with our roots firmly in the British brass band tradition, our musical range is wide — from Tudor dances, through 18th - 20th century classics and military marches, to pop and jazz arrangements and contemporary film music. Our players range from school-age to pensioners'. The modern picture is of the Band in 2012 advertising their next concert in the Advertiser.

SAGT. STURDY.
T.C.WETHERILL,   T.JEFFERSON.   RIFLE: WHEATLEY.   G.A.CROSBY.   F.E.MOOKLEDGE
(SEC.)   G.MATTRESS.   J.PEARCE
      MISS. ROBINSON.   MRS F.J.HAXBY ROBINSON   P.FRANKLAND.
W.J. COATES ESQ.   (DONOR OF CUP.)   F.J. HAXBY ROBINSON. ESQ.
(DONOR OF SHIELD.)   (PRESIDENT.)

1906 - 2006

Easingwold Rifle Club

Outside Galtres House in the early 1900s. Another centurion local club, their home is still in Galtres House, now, of course, the Galtres Centre where they have two ranges, a 25 yard x 10 lane indoor and an outside range nearby, which has 50m and 100 yard firing points. The grand opening of the VTC Rifle Range Club in Mill Field on the Crayke Road took place in 1908. The cover of the booklet celebrating the club's 100 years in 2006 forms the new picture with images of club members in various stages of its history. See also page 6. On his 1908 visit to the town Lt- General Baden Powell judged a shooting competition between members of Easingwold Rifle Club and local soldiers from Yorkshire Hussars Imperial Yeomanry 4th Battalion the Yorkshire Regiment. The Advertiser reported 'the result was a victory for the civilians, who carried off the shield with a score of 1,064, against the Hussars' 97 and the Yorkshire Regiment's 977'.

Easingwold Light Railway 1905

Opened in 1891 as a single-track branch line from Alne; at two and a half miles in length the Easingwold Light Railway was the UK's smallest and the last privately owned railway. It carried passengers (nine trains in each direction on weekdays and a Saturday night special to and from York) and goods, the former until 1948 and goods until 1957. There was a staff of twelve in the early days. The first train was known as the T'Awd Coffeepot on account of the shape of its engine. The track was taken up in 1960 and all that remains is the Station Hotel (now a private residence), after a devastating fire in 1967 (see next page). A train rushes past Alne in the modern picture on the London to Edinburgh main line.

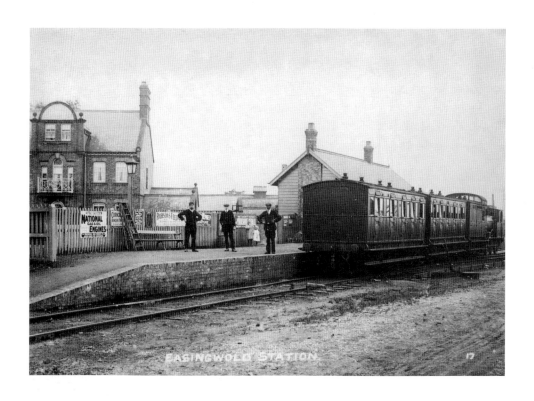

'Bad for the coo'

The early twentieth century station advertisements show a wide range of goods and services, including National Gas Engines (Ashton-under-Lyme) ; Corncrow Binder Twine; Robson's Feeds (Hull); Hall & Page, Furniture (Goodramgate, York) ; The Yorkshire Herald (York). July 14th 1900 was a memorable day in the history of the railway: The Easingwold Advertiser reports ' a venturesome beast...launched out on a voyage of discovery towards the station' and fell to the bottom of one of the 'coal shoots' resulting in 'such a bellowing and scrambling as could be heard a mile off'. The cow survived none the worse for its ordeal.

Easingwold & District Musical Society, 1903

A reproduction of the programme for the inaugural performance of the Easingwold and District Musical Society in 1903, under President Mrs Love. The lower image shows the 109-year old Easingwold Singers' latest programme, for a Christmas performance on December 3rd 2011. Dr Edwin J Crow FRCO was the first Conductor of the Society from 1903 until 1907. He was organist at Ripon Cathedral from 1873 until 1902 and founded Ripon Choral Society in 1884.

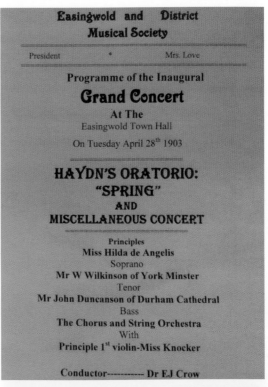

_ FANCY FAIR - JULY. 17. 07 _   EASINGWOLD PIERROT TROUPE

NORTHALLERTON
- FESTIVAL -

FESTIVAL OF BRITAIN
1851   -   -   1951

Easingwold Pierrot Troupe

At the 1907 Fancy Fair. As we have seen, Easingwold enjoys a long tradition of fairs and markets. In 1291, Earl Edmund, brother of King Edward I (Edward Longshanks and the Hammer of the Scots) instituted an annual fair here on the vigil and the feast of the Nativity of St. Mary (September 8th). In 1862 we know from the Easingwold Times of July 12th that the entertainment included a conjuror, a band, a tumbling clown sporting tights, an Aunt Sally, bazaars and cake, toffee and nut stalls. From 1946, under Alfred (Gerry) Mattinson Wilson (known as Gerry Wilson) the Singers became Easingwold Choral Society, working with other choral societies in Northallerton, Thirsk, Sutton and Leyburn. In May 2012 the Singers performed a special concert in honour of Queen Elizabeth II's jubilee, replicating in part the concert held, with Northallerton, to celebrate the 1951 Festival of Britain; Sir Edward German's Merrie England was performed in 1951, as it was in 2012.

The George

The George is eighteenth century and another Easingwold posting house on the journey to Newcastle and Edinburgh. In 1776 the cost for a post horse was 3d a mile, for a post chaise 9d and for a four horse chaise 1s 3d – this was the Newcastle Fly which travelled between the George in Coney Street, York and the Cock in Newcastle every Monday, Wednesday and Friday at 3.00pm and took the best part of a day and cost one guinea. In 1784 the Newcastle and Edinburgh Diligence took over the route. The wonderful 1885 photograph shows the horse bus which plied between Alne and Market Place before the railway opened in 1891: fare 1s either way, and five horses and three drivers were employed.

Easingwold Town AFC and the Angels

A picture of the 1911 squad. Easingwold Town was founded in 1892, the same year as Liverpool FC, only seven years after football became a professional sport and four years after the first English league was contested. Opponents in the 1899 season included Rowntree Cocoaworks, York Trinity, Stillington, Acomb, Selby, Ulleskelf, the Army Service Corps (York) and Thirsk. The new photograph shows the 2011-2012 Easingwold Angels Ladies FC squad. The Angels were formed in 2010 and play in the North Riding Women's League against such opposition as East Cleveland (Guisborough), Scarborough, Poppleton and California Ladies (sorry, that's Middlesbrough). Home gates top 100 spectators and at the time of writing they were top of the league in February 2012. L-R, back row: Manager Mark Sherwood, Kira Robinson, Emma Fawcett, Emily Jordan, GK Charlotte Simpson, GK Sonia Porter, Katie Wilkinson, Grace Holohan, Sophie Simpson, Coach Joe McGrory; front row: Jess Frith, Emma Cockerill, Liv Gillam, Captain Maz Palmer, Lauren Shuttleworth, Clara Lowther, Hannah Wade, Becky Cattley.

Selling False Teeth Through Fear

This scary advertisement from the Advertiser in 1911 tells us a lot about oral health and self image in the early days of the twentieth century. 'Life-like Artificial Teeth' and patent suction plates could not only save you from a life of ugliness but could also improve your speech and 'make eating a pleasure' – all for £1.1.0, free consultation and rail travel reimbursed for Country Patients – single teeth half a crown each. No pun intended. The new picture shows the modern face of advertising in a January 2012 Advertiser.

Mr Billy Sweep, the Loud-Voiced Talking Machine and *Stand Up Dick*

Billy Sweep was best known locally for his change from a life spent drinking heavily to becoming a devout member of the Salvation Army, swapping alcohol for copious amounts of sugar. No monument exists for Billy but there is one for John Skaife, a prominent Methodist who allowed his house to be used for meetings in the 1760s and had his windows broken for his trouble. The Bijou Theatre of Varieties came for the season in 1902 staging a repertoire which included the anticlimactic sub-titled The Midnight Express or, An Engine Driver's Story, and a 'Screaming Farce' called Stand Up Dick, which sounds more promising. In 1898 an advertisement in the Advertiser announced that Easingwold Salvationist Sgt Major Hall and a Bandsman Evans from Darlington would present the 'Monster Gramophone or Loud-Voiced Talking Machine.

The Jolly Farmers

This stood at the top of Spring Street, next to Avondale. Private Ted Webster, son of the landlord, was posted to South Africa in 1900 - an Easingwold Volunteer forming part of the King's Own Yorkshire Light Infantry. This extract from one of his letters home gives an idea of the conditions endured there: 'There is a strong Boer commando 15 miles from here, and a lot of snipers all round...the country is stinking with dead animals lying about in the veldt. Every place where we camp we have to bury some or else burn them. The whole place is infested with flies'.

MARKET PLACE, EAST, EASINGWOLD.

The Haxby Water Fountain

Erected by John Haxby's widow in 1873 in memory of her husband. Haxby was a prominent lawyer and steward of the Manor of Easingwold and Huby in 1840. Perhaps his most celebrated case was acting for the plaintiff in the 1839-49 Toll Trials. The monument is made of Polish granite; the inscription, in Latin, translates as : 'A sweet refuge for the weary wayfarer in his sweating toil'. Harry Liston, the eminent mimic ventriloquist and entertainer played the Town Hall Easingwold regularly in the 1890s with his Merry Moments; travelling shows included Bostock & Wombwell's Royal No 1 Aggregation: 'A Colossal Amalgamation of Zoological Wonders from the Uttermost Parts of the World'; it featured Wallace, King of All Lions, White Wings the Long-maned Horse, a boxing kangaroo and General Snyman, the Wonderful Mafeking Bell Ringing Ape.

The Easingwold Yeomanry

This pre World War 1 photograph of the Yeomanry was taken at the Zetland Vaults in Redcar. A poignant example of the names on the town's cenotaph is Frederick Frankland a Sapper in the 228th Field Company, Royal Engineers. He was killed in action on 7th October 1916, aged 26. Born in York, Frederick was the son of Alfred Francis and Mary Hannah Frankland, of Railway Cottages, Easingwold. He has no known grave but his name is inscribed on the Thiepval Memorial on the Somme. The new picture shows James McAvoy and Jonathan Musgrave on the set of Atonement, the Dunkirk scenes for which were filmed in Redcar in 2006.

Baden Powell and the Yeomanry 1908

The older picture shows the visit of Lt General Baden Powell as commander of the Northumbrian division of the Territorial Force. Two years later scouting in Easingwold was born when the first warrant was issued; the centenary was celebrated in 2010 with, among other events, a helicopter-assisted visit by Chief Scout Bear Grylls who paused to blow the troop's one hundred year old bugle. The first chairman and Scoutmaster was Harry Bannister, who promised that his scouts would be trained to save lives "in case of fire, sewer gas, ice breaking, runaway horses, drowning, etc." Katherine Love gave Easingwold its first scout hut. The new photograph was published in the Advertiser in 2012 and pictures the 1st Moxby Moor cub Scouts working towards their chef badges in activities which included making pizzas at the New Inn, Huby.

Bank House, Market Place

All decked out for the coronation of Edward VIIth: God Bless King & Queen. The notice in the window on the left next to the door says 'Yorkshire Banking Co. Ltd. Open 10 to 3, Friday 10 to 4, Saturday 10 to 12'. The one to the left of that 'Post Office' and above that to the left 'Parcel Post Office'. The new picture shows the White House in Market Place.

Mark Reynard – Ironmonger and Bicycle Agent

Another famous Easingwold business noted for its bicycles at the turn of the twentieth century: apart from stocking models like Swift (£10.10.0), Flying Arrow (£9.10.0) and Lady's Goodby (£5.10.0) they also gave cycling lessons and offered a free inflating service. Guns, ammunition and sewing machines were also available and motor cycles could be built to order; they were also quick to meet the demand for lamps after the new vehicle (carriages and carts) lighting regulations were introduced in 1900. Reynard's later became a garage and then a bus company. Frank Reynard is the grandfather of Adrian Reynard, motorcycle and racing car driver and builder.

'Learn or Leave !'

The poster on the building at the front on the left was a Royal Navy recruiting poster. To the right is the National School which flourished from 1862 and included in its intake seven boys and girls from poor families and provided a free education for them. It now houses the library; the uncompromising inscription above the main door reads 'Learn or Leave' , although the Compulsory Education Act certainly outlawed such a stark choice. The good works of the National Society for Promoting the Education of the Poor in the Principles of the Established Church were responsible for Easingwold National School, despite its pithy title.

Uppleby and Nana Randan

Tudor House still stands here (see page 54) and a thatched Tudor public house, the Blue Bell, now demolished, was run by Anne Harrison, better known as Nana Randan. She was permitted by her friend Thomas Salvin to use the 'chief seat' in the parish church. Her grave is near to the church door; legend has it that if at midnight you run round the church three times and spit on it she will rise from her grave. The Jolly Farmers nearby also had a thatched roof.

The Smith's

This fascinating 1899 photograph pictures Reginald Ernest Smith, Editor of the Easingwold Advertiser on the far right with his future wife, Annie Elizabeth Coates, Bell Coates on the left and Ellen Coates on the right – she played Britannia in the Boer War parades. The other picture shows the front page from an edition of the Advertiser from October 1899. Note the advertisements for Tiny Tots magazine and King's Vital Restorative Pilules for 'Weak Men'; efficacious in 'Failing Memory, Trembling Sensations, Exhausted Vitality, Premature Decline, Feeling of 'Worn Out', Palpitation, Skin Eruption, Piles, Kidney and Bladder Affections, Discharges'.

Tudor House, Uppleby

This early to mid 17th century building in the new photograph is notable as being the only visible timber framed house left in the town. Internally, it retains its timbered smoke hood, a predecessor to the brick chimney. Gill in Vallis Eboracensis reports that 'only a few thatched and timbered buildings survived even in his time' (1852) and cites the 'God With Us' House in Spring Street, two others in Uppleby (one of which is in the old picture here) and Shepherd's Garth in Long Street.

How To Rule A Wife

In 1834 Pigot's Directory lists three schools in Uppleby: William Hardcastle's; Ann Mountain's and Francis Rowling's. Trades here included six boot and shoe makers, one bricklayer, three cartwrights, a hairdresser and a maltster, four grocers, a tailor, a cooper, a brewer and a surgeon – all indicating that it was a much more commercial area than it is today. As we have seen, Easingwold could support a theatre and welcomed itinerants: in December 1811 'Their Majesties Servants' – a company of fourteen including three children - put on The Stranger, or, Misanthropy and Repentance during which Dolly Duggins sang a recital, followed by Phantasmogoria starring Macbeth, Lord Nelson and Osman Pasvanoglu, the Widdin of Bulgaria. Later productions included The Ghost, or the Affrighted Farmer, a 'Melo Dramatic Spectacle' and The Honey Moon, or How to Rule a Wife.

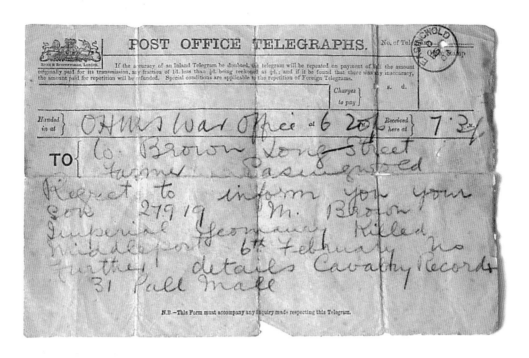

*Poppies and Wreath Card which was sent for the
100th Anniversary of the Battle of Middlepost*

100th Anniversary 5th & 6th February 1902

THE BATTLE AT MIDDLEPOST

In memory of the brave British and Boer soldiers who were
killed in action here. Also to the four soldiers of the Imperial
Yeomanry who took part in the battle and came from the small
market town of Easingwold in North Yorkshire:-

MARK KNOWLSON BROWN
ARTHUR BOWMAN
TED SPENCE
FRANK WEIGHELL

In Remembrance

Donated by the people of Easingwold

The War Telegram

The telegram sent from the War Office to Mr
Wm Brown, farmer, of Long Street, the father
of Trooper Mark Knowlson Brown informing
them that he had been killed at Middlepost,
Cape Colony on February 6th 1902, 'no
further details'. Trooper Brown was serving
with the 11th Imperial Yeomanry; a memorial
service was held later that month and then a
letter was received from him dated eight days
after his alleged death. It had all been a terrible
mistake and Trooper Brown returned home to
a hero's welcome in August 1902. The other
image shows the wreath and wreath card
donated by the people of Easingwold on the
100th anniversary of the Battle of Middlepost.

GH Smith, Easingwold

Over the years GH Smith has published a number of facsimiles of important works that have been out of print, thus rescuing them from obscurity and ensuring continued availability. Amongst these are the famous Illustrated Michelin Guides to the Battlefields (1914-1918). The photograph shows a house advertisement for The Michelin Hospital which describes the fully staffed and equipped military hospital established and paid for by the company in London. By the end of the war it had treated 2,993 wounded soldiers. This is taken from 'Ypres' as are the lower pages showing the British cemetery at the Hospice Notre-Dame and (lower) the Menin Gate.

MICHELIN DURING THE WAR

THE MICHELIN HOSPITAL

When the Great War broke out, Michelin at once converted an immense new four-storied warehouse into an up-to-date Hospital, with Operating Theatre, X-Ray, Bacteriological Laboratory, etc. Seven weeks later (September 22, 1914) Doctors, Dispensers, Nurses, Sisters of Mercy, and auxiliaries were all at their posts. The first wounded arrived the same night. In all, 2,993 wounded were received.

All expenses were paid by Michelin.

The story of how Michelin did "his bit" during the war is told briefly and simply in the illustrated booklet, "The Michelin Hospital," sent post free on application.

A VIEW OF ONE OF THE WARDS.

MICHELIN & Cie., Clermont-Ferrand, France.
MICHELIN TYRE Co., Ltd., 81, Fulham Road, London, S.W. 3.

FACSIMILE OF ORIGINAL ADVERT – The information given is NOT relevant today.

53

102

ARMENTIÈRES. NÔTRE DAME CHURCH WAS NOT GREATLY DAMAGED BY THE BOMBARDMENTS (*see below*)

Visit the ruins of **St. Waast Church,** *then return to Rue de Dunkerque. There take the first street on the right and cross the Lys. From the Bridge there is a general view of the church.*

BRITISH CEMETERY AT THE HOSPICE NÔTRE-DAME

are decorated with flamboyant figures. These tympana were added some years later, thus giving the wide 17th century windows, of which the (French) architect of the Hôtel Merghelynck made such happy use (photo, p. 101).

Having reached the Grande-Place, take the Rue de Menin on the right, leaving on the left the ruins of the Hospice Nôtre-Dame. Next take the Menin Road, to visit the Château de Hooge and **Zillebeke.**

ARMENTIÈRES. NÔTRE-DAME CHURCH, WHICH THE GERMANS BLEW UP BEFORE BEING DRIVEN OUT OF THE TOWN (*see above*)

MENIN GATE
On leaving Ypres in the direction of Hooge and Zillebeke.

57

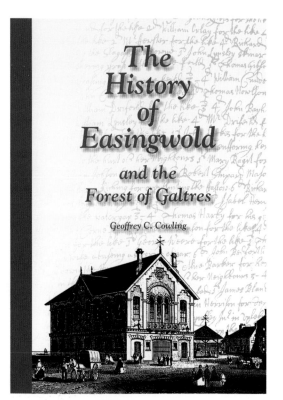

Thomas Gill, Book Printer and Publisher

The Advertiser follows in a long tradition of Easingwold newspaper publishing stretching back to 1854 when Thomas Gill set up the The Easingwold Chronicle and North Riding Advertiser, renamed and expanded in 1855 under the banner The Easingwold Times; preferring something a little less punchy he soon changed it again to The Easingwold Chronicle & Thirsk Times Advertiser. Thomas Gill was also a book printer and publisher of some note with his printing works in Chapel Street and then Market Place. Gill died a pauper in the 1870s. Geoffrey Cowling's The History of Easingwold and the Forest of Galtres is another important work reprinted by GH Smith. From the Vale to the Veldt is an important history of Easingwold's involvement in the Boer War which provides an excellent history of the town seen largely through the pages and photographs of the Easingwold Advertiser.

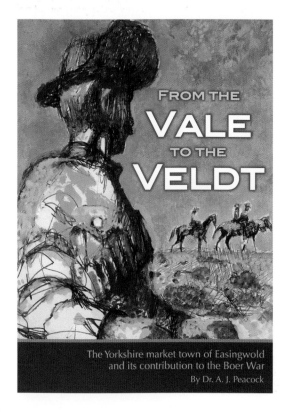

Vallis Eboracensis : Comprising the History & Antiquities of Easingwold and the Forest of Galtres

The old picture shows Market Place in the sixties. Gill gives us some interesting information on Easingwold industry in the mid nineteenth century, telling us that the 'principle manufacture is that of Steels, for which it has long been celebrated, both on the continent of Europe, and the states of America. It is also famous for its bacon and butter, great quantities of which are sent to York and London'. Weaving, he adds, was a thing of the past here. Gill was a much better author and historian than newspaper magnate: in 1862 he sold the title to John and Joseph Smith who promptly renamed it The Easingwold Times eventually selling it with the printing machinery to Leonard and George Smith (1844-1898).

Market Place and The Commercial

The fine houses on the west of Market Place (Croft, Rocliffe and Prospect Houses are visible in the newer photograph), the old vicarage, the old National School and the Commercial Inn can all be seen in this old photograph which encapsulates the essence of Edwardian village life. Not that much has changed in 2012.

St John the Baptist & All Saints

It was effectively the Archdeacons of Richmond Thomas Dalby and Stephen le Scrope who rebuilt the church between 1388 to 1418 retaining only the Raskelf Door and the West Window to produce the church we largely see today.

The Fleece Inn

George Smith was also Easingwold's postmaster, ropemaker, and innkeeper of the Fleece Inn on Long Street. In 1867 the Times was closed down and the brothers concentrated solely on printing. In 1870 George moved his Post Office to the Market Place – on the site of what became the Yorkshire Bank, today's HSBC Bank, where he also sold wines and spirits and…pianos. His Bremmer Printing Works (named after the huge gas-powered printing presses) were set up in the cottages behind – down the ginnel known as the 'Post Office Slip'. George's son, Reginald Ernest Smith, published the first true Advertiser'in January 1892 under the title The Easingwold Advertiser and Weekly News. The first newspaper to be distributed in the town was the weekly York Mercury from March 1718; a collection of articles from the London press with a few local advertisements it was bought by the eccentric Thomas Gent in 1724 and retitled as the catchy The Original York Journal, or Weekly Courant, later simply the York Courant.

Easingwold School

Nowadays Easingwold primary school children attend what was the Grammar School on Thirsk Road, built in 1911. The first building here, the Tin Tabernacle, was erected in 1905. Easingwold School built in 1954 now educates 1350 students on the York Road as a Specialist Language College. The photographs show an early mathematics exercise book and a scene from a 1962 school production of Toad of Toad Hall, all looking a bit serious. The book was William Slinger's from June 1912.

Eleanor Westerman

Easingwold School all started with Eleanor Westerman's 1781 will which provided £2,500 for a charity school for thirty boys and thirty girls of Easingwold to be taught 'freely' a range of subjects which included Latin and bookkeeping. The older picture shows the school's very first assembly in the new school on York Road in 1954. The new photograph is of the dedicated Sixth Form Centre.

Easingwold School Girls' Cricket XI

The 1913 Girl's Cricket team. The new picture was published in the Easingwold Advertiser ninety-nine years later and shows that cricket amongst girls is alive and well, under the auspices of the Forest of Galtres Cricket Development Group – set up to encourage local girls to practice and play the game and form a CDG team.

Mensuration and Surveying

The old picture shows the 1881 Grammar School's first building – not much more than a farm cottage – in Back Lane behind 'Allenville'. It grew out of the Westerman Grammar School then at the Thirsk end of Long Street (now Barton and Westerman Houses, see next page) and later Longley House. Apart from the usual three 'r's the curriculum included Mensuration and Surveying.

The 1888 Prize List

A fascinating glimpse of the Grammar School curriculum for 1888; Mr and Mrs Woodward must have been particularly proud. Latin and Greek were reintroduced in 1892 with Euclid, Algebra, Trigonometry, French, Physiology and Drawing. Chemistry, Music and Shorthand came in 1898.

Easingwold Grammar School,

1888.

PRIZE · LIST.

Holy Scripture (and Highest Proficiency) Vicar's Prize.	W. Woodward.
High Proficiency in the Annual Examination Hon. P. Dawnay's Prize.	A. W. Beasley.
High Proficiency	H. Woodward.
Science	T. Wilkinson.
Holy Scripture and General Proficiency	T. H. Jones.
Mathematics	R. Cowling.

SUCCESSES DURING THE YEAR.

London Matriculation – {	T. Harrison. H. L. Ratcliffe.	1st Division. do.
Preliminary Pharmaceutical		Wm. Maskew.

SCIENCE and ART DEPARTMENT.

Chemistry - A. Bensley, T. Jones, W. Woodward, H. Woodward, W. Maskew, A. Sturdy, T. Wilkinson.

Agriculture - A. Sturdy, W. Woodward, H. Woodward, T. Wilkinson, T. Jones, G. Plummer.

Mathematics - A. Bensley, W. Woodward, H. Woodward, T. Jones.

Freehand Drawing (2nd Grade) - G. Plummer.

In addition to the above, ten other Certificates have been gained by Mr. Davis' private pupils, from the London University, Institute of Bankers, College of Preceptors and Science and Art Department.

'A Seminary for Young Ladies'

Other local schools from the Victorian era included 'a seminary for young ladies' at Spring Head House in Spring Street later in 1890 moving to Longley House in Long Street; this was run by Misses EA and FK Blyth with the assistance of Fraulein Koch from Bavaria. The Roman Catholic elementary day school opened in 1871 next to the Roman Catholic church.

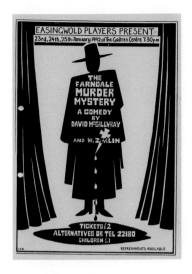

EASINGWOLD
PLAYERS

From Mother Figure to Waiting in the Wings

Easingwold Players was formed in 1989 by Barbara Topping; her inaugural productions were the Alan Ayckbourn plays Mother Figure and Gosforth's Fete in the Galtres Centre on 21 and 22 April 1989. Barbara is still acting and performed in the Players' latest production, Noel Coward's Waiting in the Wings. The pictures show how far programme design and production have moved on in the twenty-three years of the Players' life: the basic photocopy has given way to full colour programmes sponsored through generous advertising by local businesses.

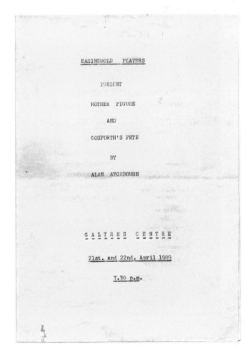

Please sir, I want some more. What ?

When the new Galtres sports hall was built in 2008 the original sports hall was converted into a fully equipped auditorium which Easingwold Players christened with a spectacular production of Oliver ! So popular were the auditions that Directors Loretta Knaggs and Abbigail Wright set up a Red Team and a Blue Team resulting in a cast of 112! Paul Dyson was the Musical Director and led a thirteen-part orchestra. The pictures show another splendid programme and a superb photograph of the dress rehearsals.

Well I will not grow up! You cannot make me!

November 2010 saw Abbigail Wright's production of JM Barrie's Peter Pan. Barrie's original script was used for the production which meant that the licence fee was paid to Great Ormond Street Children's Hospital to which Barrie had bequeathed the rights for Peter Pan. The play saw the first time actors and actresses flew from the Galtres Centre stage! Laura Soper (here in the photo) and Thomas Lister went on to re-create their roles of Wendy and Michael Darling in the York Theatre Royal production, winning rave reviews in The Times.

EASINGWOLD PLAYERS PRESENT

PETER PAN

A PLAY BY J.M. BARRIE

November 2010

The Farndale Avenue Housing Estate Townswomen's Guild Dramatic Society Murder Mystery

The poster for this 1992 production and the dress rehearsal for the latest production, Waiting in the Wings, from November 2011. No less that fifty-six productions have been staged since 1989. The programme for 2012 is Winnie the Pooh in April and Alan Ayckbourn's Seasons Greetings in November.

CHAPTER TWO: AROUND EASINGWOLD

Robert Thompson and Ampleforth Abbey

The work of Kilburn's Robert Thompson can be seen all over Yorkshire and indeed Britain. His favourite commission is reputedly the carvings he did in the library of Ampleforth College where he worked from the 1920s to the 1950s when he retired. One of his earlier commissions was the wooden cross which stands in the graveyard at Ampleforth Abbey. This came about after a meeting with Father Paul Nevill, a monk at the abbey and parish priest in Ampleforth village, which also resulted in a refrectory table and a chair for Ampleforth College, both still in use today. A Thompson refrectory table today will cost you over £8000. The old picture shows Ampleforth College from the east, around 1910.

Ampleforth Abbey and its Dissolutions

An 1802 view of Ampleforth's original 1783 building. The Abbey of St Laurence, Ampleforth is Britain's biggest Benedictine community; seventy-eight men live here according to the Rule of St. Benedict under an Abbot. It is a vowed life of prayer and work: ora et labora. Ampleforth has its origins in the monastery re-established in Westminster Abbey by Mary Tudor, although this was dissolved for a second time (after Henry VIII) by Elizabeth I. At the end of the eighteenth century Fr Anselm Bolton, former chaplain of Lady Anne Fairfax at Gilling Castle, moved into Ampleforth Lodge which Lady Anne had built for him. In 1802 Fr Anselm gave the house over to a number of Benedictines who had fled Dieulouard in Lorraine after the Revolution; this was to be their new monastery; in 1803 the new monastery school opened.

Ampleforth Missions

Over the next hundred years or so the monks worked not only in the college but also on missions in the new town parishes thrown up by the industrial revolution - in South Wales, Liverpool and Warrington around Preston and in Cumbria. The older picture shows some of the monks in the early 1900s; the modern photograph is of Fr Kentigern Hagan, Warden of the Visitor Centre at Ampleforth Abbey in 2012.

Arriving at Ampleforth

The old photograph shows and anxious looking eleven year old Reginald Marwood arriving in his father's Renault in 1901. All turned out well – he became Fr Stephen, house master of St Oswald's. Ampleforth has had, since 1918, one of the six Oxford Permanent Private Halls at St Benet's Hall founded in 1897. It is mainly but not exclusively for training priests enabling them to read for secular degrees. Benet's is the last remaining part of the university admitting only men. In 1955 Ampleforth established a sister priory in St. Louis, Missouri – the Priory of Saints Mary and Louis. In 1996, the community of Christ the Word in Zimbabwe was set up: four or five members of the community are there at any one time and the present Abbot spends at least three months of the year at this monastery.

Ampleforth OTC

The old photograph shows the Ampleforth College Officer Training Corps on a 1936 post card sent to Miss KM Walls from Peter, the sergeant in the foreground at camp in Aldershot and about to go on night operations. Old Boys include Cardinal Basil Hume, Grand Duke Jean of Luxembourg (b. 1921); King Letsie III of Lesotho (b. 1963); Paul Moore, whistleblower sacked from HBOS; Piers Paul Read; Rupert Everett and Lawrence Dallaglio. The new picture is of part of the Abbey's splendid Visitor's Centre.

Ampleforth Village

A 1930s view of the village main street. The new photograph shows the Wesleyan Chapel. Ampleforth also had a Quaker settlement in Shallowdale; Flax workers lived in the 16th century Carr House Farm, now a guest house.

'One of the shining lights of northern monasticism'

In his Historia Rerum Anglicarum William of Newburgh, an Augustinian canon at Newburgh, described Byland Abbey as 'one of the shining lights of northern monasticism' after the monks settled there in 1177. At its peak it was one of the largest of the Savigniac order abbeys in Britain. The marauding Scots laid it waste after the battle of Shaws Moor in 1322 and Henry VIII dissolved it in 1538 after which it quickly fell into disrepair and became a source of stone for local buildings. Abbot Phillip's 1197 Historia Fundationis gives us much of the early history of Byland Abbey.

The Savigniacs

The Savigniacs were one of the monastic orders which, in the late 11th and early 12th centuries, emerged based on the Rule of St Benedict. The most famous were the Cistercians, founded in 1098 at Cîteaux in Burgundy. Less well known were the Savigniacs, founded 1112, from Savigny in Normandy who merged with the Cistercian order in 1147. The Savigniacs came to England and founded their first house at Tulketh near Preston in 1124, soon moving to Furness in Cumbria in 1128. Their main patron was Stephen, Count of Boulogne and Mortain, king of England from 1135. After a short stay at Hood near Sutton Bank and five years at Oldstead, the Savigniacs came to Byland around 1155 spending the next twenty years clearing the marshy site and draining the land in preparation for the building of the abbey.

Byland Abbey and the Scots

Edward II invaded Scotland in 1322 retreating after burning the Cistercian abbey at Melrose only to be pursued by the army of Robert the Bruce which camped at Shaws Moor near Byland. Edward was at Rievaulx and the Scots ruthlessly attacked Byland and followed the English king to Pickering, Bridlington and York. By 1391, plague reduced numbers to eleven monks and three lay brothers. 1538 saw the abbey dissolved by Henry VIII; Abbot Alanbrig and twenty-five monks received their pensions; the plate was taken to London with other moveables and the buildings were stripped of lead, glass and timber. Byland was relatively fortunate – the Abbot at the daughter house of Jervaulx was hung, drawn and quartered for his involvement in the Pilgrimage of Grace.

Byland Abbey and the Stapyltons of Myton Hall

The Stapyltons of Myton Hall owned the abbey for many years. In 1819 Martin Stapylton excavated the church and the chapter house in the hope of finding the grave of Roger de Mowbray. Tons of stone were removed to Myton Hall along with the high altar slab and an alabaster image of the Trinity; both are now in Ampleforth Abbey. Byland was sold in 1893 to the Newburgh Estate which still owns the site today.

Shandy Hall, Coxwold

Once a priest's house in the Middle Ages this was home for Laurence Sterne (b. 1713) for the last eight years of his life. He wrote A Sentimental Journey Through France and Italy and Sermons of Mr Yorick here as well as seven of the nine volumes of The Life and Opinions of Tristram Shandy here. Shandy Hall is now a museum housing, among other things, the world's largest collection of Sterne's manuscripts and first editions.

CXD.3 THE VILLAGE, COXWOLD

Copyright Frith's

Laurence Sterne and the Resurrection Men

Sterne died of pleurisy in London in 1768; he was buried in the churchyard in Coxwold but only after a circuitous journey... He was originally interred in St George's churchyard, Hanover Square, London, but his body was snatched by 'resurrection men' for use in medical dissection at Cambridge University. The cadaver was recognised by the Professor of Anatomy who fainted when he saw it on the table and had it hastily reburied. In 1969 the Laurence Sterne Society obtained permission to remove Sterne's remains to Coxwold for re- burial . Published over 10 years from 1759-1769 The Life and Opinions of Tristram Shandy, Gentleman soon came to be regarded to be as one of the great comic novels in the English language. The pub here on the right, the Fauconberg Arms, is named after the Fauconberg Hospital, a 1662 almhouse for "ten poor and infirm men", now old people's homes. The pub sign bears the somewhat self- deprecating Fauconberg motto: "Bonne et Belle Assez".

Coxwold and Mary Cromwell

Laurence Sterne was parson at the 15th century St Michael's Church which stands on the site of a Norman predecessor. Among its treasures are its octagonal tower, a 16th century Spanish sword forged in Toledo, a copy of the Geneva Bible printed in 1601 (the Breeches Bible) in a case made by Robert Thompson, coloured bosses and 15th century glass. Mary Cromwell, Oliver's daughter, who married Thomas Ballasis, first Earl of Fauconberg, is buried here. The older photograph from 1899 shows the party on page 53 to have moved on to the pub at Coxwold – RE Smith is at the back of the cart.

Cucwald

A number of houses in the village bear the crest and monogram of Sir George Ormby Wombwell. The Colvils became Lords of the Manor here after the Conquest. Old Hall was originally the Grammar School built in 1603 by Sir John Harte from Kilburn. Harte went to London as an apprentice grocer, married his master's daughter and became Lord Mayor of London. The school closed in 1894 and is now a private house. The origin of Coxwold is Cuhu walda: Cuhu is a personal name and walda is a wood. To the Normans it was Cucwald: cuc meaning to crow as cock's do.

Newburgh Hall, Coxwold

Newburgh Priory was founded in 1145 as an Augustinian Friary by Roger de Mowbray after his father, Robert, was granted the lands by William the Conqueror. Newburgh is unusual in that has remained in the ownership of one family - from Sir William Bellasis, who converted it into a private residence in 1546, to Captain and Mrs Wombwell, owners until 1986. Henry VIII had sold Newburgh to one of his chaplains, Anthony de Bellasis, for £1,062. Newburgh remained in the possession of the Bellasis family until 1825; they took the title of Fauconberg in 1627.

The Headless Oliver Cromwell

Margaret Tudor stayed here on 17 August 1503 on the way to meet her husband, James IV of Scotland . Oliver Cromwell (minus his head) was reputedly entombed by Mary, his daughter, in a bricked up attic room . A silver screw-top pen bearing his initials is there; whether he is, is another matter... The old picture shows the Coxwold church funeral of Sir George Wombwell of Newburgh Priory, October 1913. Wombwell had been Chairman of the Honourable East India Company and was MP for Huntingdon from 1774 to 1780.

Easingwold Rifle and Pistol Club (British Legion) 1963

Above: Coxwold Outdoor Range 1979

The Coxwold Outdoor Range

These pages are taken from the booklet produced by the Easingwold Rifle club to celebrate 100 years in 2006 and show the club at various stages of its history. Sir George Wombwell opened the Coxwold range in 1981 – a section of disused railway cutting had been leased for fifteen years from Captain Victor Malcolm Wombwell and a 100 yard purpose built range including club room, covered firing point.

Dr Slop: a scene from Laurence Sterne's *The Life and Opinions of Tristram Shandy, Gentleman*

The Hogarth sketch shows Dr Slop snoozing in the parlour at Shandy Hall as Corporal Trim reads the Sermon. Dr Slop was based on a Dr John Burton who lived in the Red House in York, now an antiques centre. Burton was a gynaecologist and writer; his books included An Essay Towards a Complete System of Midwifery, illustrated by no less an artist than George Stubbs who had come to York to learn his anatomy. Stubbs ended up teaching medical students before moving on to perfecting his comparative anatomy and painting his famous horses. The LNER poster is from the 1930s and by Austin Cooper; it shows characters from the novel outside Shandy Hall.

The Church & Hall, CRAYKE.

The Church of St Cuthbert in Crayke

Mostly dates from around 1490 although the north aisle was added in 1863. Edward Churton, theologian and Hispanic scholar was rector from 1835; the average number of villagers attending Crayke church services in 1865 was around 200, thirty of whom were communicants. Churton tells us that a typical Sunday congregation in 1865 was 300 – over half the total population of the village. He noted 'some cases of irreligion and immorality' which were 'I trust, not on the increase.' The south wall has grooves in it which were made by the sharpening of arrows by future conscripts in the English army.

Crayke Castle

A wooden motte and bailey Norman castle probably stood on the site first, later rebuilt in stone. Most of it was dilapidated by the early 16th century and little remains today. The present castle is from around 1450 , built by Bishop Neville. King John stayed here in 1209, 1210 and 1211, Henry III in 1227, Edward I in 1292, Edward II in 1316 and Edward III in 1345. Parliament destroyed the castle in 1646; by 1780 it was being used as a farmhouse. Water for the castle was carried or pumped up from the village well; mains water started flowing up the hill in the 1920s. The castle was used as a billet for the Women's Land Army during World War II.

Bishop's Cottage

There is evidence of Roman activity here with the most significant being a large stone building along with roundhouses, metalworking paraphernalia and a kiln. The building which measures thirty metres by ten includes a portico and may well perhaps have been a British temple. Cuthbert, later Bishop of Lindesfarne (c. 634-687), was granted Crayke (Saxon Creca) and the surrounding land to an extent of three miles by Ecgfrid, the Saxon king of Northumbria; it then served as a resting place for Cuthbert on his journeys between Lindesfarne and York. The timber framed cottage from 1615 on the left, Bishop's Cottage, was demolished, reputedly on the orders of Miss Mathews who lived in the Hall, because it spoilt her view down the hill.

Quaker Persecution

Page, in his A History of the County of York North Riding: Volume 2 (1923), tells us that 'the new Wesleyan chapel has an ancient crowned shield, bearing the sacred monogram, built into the front wall. It was probably brought from Marton Priory'. This is the old chapel built in 1787 in School Street. In 1801 it had twenty members. The new chapel closed in 1902 and became a private house taking the name Whistling Green. Quakers were not tolerated in Crayke despite the presence of a Meeting house in 1689: they were deemed unfitting to have their names listed along with 'true Christians'.

A Hen for Christmas

Being under the ownership of the Bishop of Durham (as a peculier) Crayke won a reputation as a safe haven for outlaws, the local magistrate having no jurisdiction; this anomaly was only remedied when Crayke joined the North Riding in 1844. The Diocese Book of 1793 states that there were ninety houses in Crayke, all occupied by farmers and labourers except John Bowman Esq. and the rector Thomas Bowman . 'Every house pays a hen at Christmas or else sixpence' and 'Everyone pays 2d for his or her Easter offering who then receives ye Blessed Sacrament of ye Lord's Supper'. In the old photograph the 16th century Tudor cottage is on the left with Oak Cottage next door displaying the shop of J Gibson, Tailor & Draper, Dealer in Fancy Goods, Stationery.

The Village Schools

Churton and Dr Henry Yates Whytehead MD (son of the missionary and poet, Thomas Whytehead), put up the money for the building of the first village school house in 1846. Whytehead lived next door to the church in what is now Crayke Hall. The Illustrated London News of 1 Feb. 1846 pictured and described the school. The opening was a grand event which included lunch for the seventy-two children of the parish, after a service in St Cuthbert's. When the new primary school opened in 1972 it was used as the village hall (as the Churton Hall) for some twenty years and is now a private house, on West Way. The bell tower was struck by lightning in the 1971 and never replaced.

The Durham Ox

The Durham Ox, AA pub of the year in 2008, was a notable hostelry on the drover's road from Scotland to the meat markets of the south and London. Page lists some fascinating place names extant in the manor in 1648: Nyne Penny Piece, Fower Megge Flatte, Heather Intacke ,Crooke Inge, Fosse Flatt, Two Sam Peeces, Slee Close, Great and Little Hagg Inge, Weight Land, Bulpitt, Mart Gate Inge, Oxeclose, Sir Richard Close, Overfossette, Claude, Fetherstons and Cow Close. All very descriptive of a rural community dependent on agriculture.

Molly Webster and Mabel Thornton

Crayke's other (long gone) pub was the Rose & Crown, seen here to the left , up the hill, of the 1902 Methodist chapel. It was known locally as The Crown, and before that was named The Greyhound. A third pub is named in an 1820 trade directory: The Horse & Hounds. Two earlier chapels predated this one: one on School Street built in 1787 and one on Key Lane from 1852. Crayke can boast two witches: Molly Webster practiced her infernal arts mainly on cows whose milk she turned sour although she was known to stab people with her pins; Mabel Thornton was the other.

Helperby and Brafferton

A fine Francis Frith shot of Helperby Main Street showing bakers and window cleaner on the right and The Golden Lion on the left. Brafferton is older than Helperby and was probably settled by the Romans - the Roman road from Malton (Derventio) to Aldborough (Isurium) passed nearby to cross the river Swale by ford, hence the name: Brafferton = brad - ford - tun, the town at the broad ford. Domesday mentions that Brafferton has a church and a priest in Brafferton Ancient rectory, Patronage of Riparia.

The River Jordan of England

The old picture shows a laden horse and cart outside Brafferton Manor. Pre-conquest Brafferton was renowned for its connection with St Paulinus, disciple of St Augustine and first Bishop of York, who converted Edwin, the Saxon king of Northumbria, to Christianity and used the river Swale here as a place of baptism. Allegedly in 626 at Christmas 10,000 people went into the river to be Christened, with no casualties despite the numbers. Indeed, those with a "feeblenesse and infirmitie" re-emerged "whole and reformed". This, and similar mass baptisms in the region, for example Catterick, led to the Swale being christened the River Jordan of England.

Anyone for Marbles ?

A delightful picture of Brafferton schoolboys preoccupied by a serious game of marbles in 1910 – closely observed by the policeman, predicting a riot no doubt. The school on the right burnt down in 1943. Ralph Rymer was Lord of the Brafferton Manor in 1641; their son, Thomas, became a barrister, translator, critic and poet. To Alexander Pope he was 'one of the best critics we ever had' but to Thomas Macaulay he was 'the worst critic who ever lived'. We might perhaps sympathise with Macaulay when we learn that Rymer believed that Shakespeare had no genius for tragedy and considered Othello ' a bloody farce without salt or savour'.

The Fountain and Dunroyal, Helperby

The Fountain was built in 1897 to commemorate Queen Victoria's Diamond Jubilee , an honour now shared with the centenary of Lady Celia Milnes-Coates of Helperby Hall. Note the hayloft in the building on the right. Dunroyal is on the left. When Robert Boyle (he of the famous physics Law) died in 1691 his executors were charged with using the proceeds of his estate to spread the Christian word amongst 'infidels'; land was duly bought, including Brafferton Manor, and their rents went towards the construction of the Brafferton Building at the College of William & Mary in Williamsburg, Virginia in 1723 for the education of native Indian children under the aegis of the Society for Advancing the Christian Faith amongst the Infidels of the British Colonies in America, later the Society for the Conversion and Religious Instruction and Education of the Negro Slaves in the British West India Islands, and later still with an even less pithy name, too long to record here; suffice to say that the CFS, as it became known, has left its mark in Brafferton with a plaque outside Brafferton School and the initials CFS engraved on the facades or gable ends of a number of the village's houses.

The Gallant Band of Five

Robert Leadley is pictured here with sons William and Lawrence in Fountain House, Dunroyal. The other local joiner was Frankland's set up by Edwin at the rear of Brafferton House in the late 1800s; opposite was Brown's the blacksmiths in Hall Lane. World War I claimed thirty villagers' lives including two nurses and the Gallant Band of Five. These were five territorials in the 4th Btn Yorkshire Regiment who were sent up the line near Ypres in April 1915 to reinforce Canadian and Algerian troops who had just endured the first gas attack in the history of war. The Algerians had fled leaving the line exposed but the Canadians and the Yorkshire recaptured St Julien in the face of German infantry, artillery and mustard gas attacks. A shell exploded above the trench and killed five Helperby soldiers.

Brafferton Manor Farm

The 1841 census highlights the obvious local dependency on farming: thirty farmers, eighty-seven farm labourers, a farmer's hand, a horse breaker, a cattle dealer, six blacksmiths, a saddler, a drayman and a wheelwright with three apprentices. Other tradespeople included three butchers, ten shoemakers, four tailors, a basketmaker, a straw bonnet maker, three brickmakers and a tinner. There were seventy-two servants, a Ladies' Seminary Keeper in Brafferton House with fifteen girls under age sixteen in her care and three twenty-year old girls living in as assistants.

Helperby-cum-Rugeley

A break in filming in a Helperby that had been adapted by Yorkshire TV in 1998 to look like Rugeley, Staffordshire in the 1840s; this was for a film about the notorious poisoner William Palmer — quite coincidently the namesake of the surveyor who developed the navigation of the River Swale here in 1736 . To feed his gambling habit Palmer poisoned members of his family and claimed the insurance; he was hanged at Stafford in 1856. The surgery became the corn mill, Vine Cottage the forge, aerials were removed and traffic was banned.

The Pumpkin Club

The Oak Tree Inn was the venue in 1989 when the Helperby & Brafferton Pumpkin Club was formed. Marrows and sunflowers were allowed in in 1992; each year the annual show is held alternately in one of the villages' pubs. Helperby has a strong tradition in brewing with the Lambert brewery from 1823 and Ramsden's Brewery in Main Street which survives as the house named The Old Brewery. Ramsden bought the Lamberts out in 1875 and in 1926 purchased the Castle Brewery at Sheriff Hutton with its tied houses. In 1876 there was a brewery in Back Lane, the Back Lane Brewery, later the Star Brewery after The Star Inn there. The Maltings operated off Bridge Street from the early 1800s until the 1970s. the newer photograph shows Helperby Hall built, somewhat eccentrically, in 1900; the inscription above the door reads… Les Marionettes Font, font, font Trois petits tours Et puis s'en vont.

The Golden Lion, Helperby

The sign on the side of the building reads JH Scaife, Joiner and Cabinetmaker, Printer. The three surviving pubs in Helperby and the one in Brafferton are all that is left of the fourteen which used to serve the two villages – an indicator of the busy commercial activity that used to take place here in what was a terminus at the navigable section of the Swale. Dales pack horse trails also passed through the villages, bringing trade in grain and wool. The pubs included The Greyhound (or The Dog) – now a private house, Woodlands; The Unicorn in Bridge Street once owned by the Leadley family; The Star in Back Lane, now Old Star Cottage; The Rose & Crown in what is now Raskelf Road, closed by John Smith's in 1970; the Half Moon. The Golden Lion destroyed in the Great Fire and rebuilt, The Oak Tree and The Farmer's Inn (The Fox Inn) all survive.

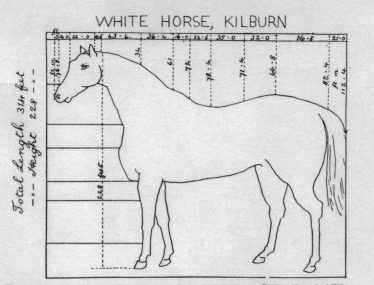

WHITE HORSE, KILBURN

The above is a reduced copy of the original plan from which the famous "White Horse" of Kilburn was constructed in 1857. The plan was made by Mr. John Hodgson, then schoolmaster at Kilburn, who superintended the execution of the scheme for making this notable Yorkshire landmark.

The White Horse, Kilburn

With an eye big enough to fit twenty people into it, the celebrated horse on Roulston Scar is 304 feet long, 228 feet high and covers two acres. 'Delivered' in 1857 by John Hodgson, the village school master and sometime surveyor, with the help of thirty-three local men, the lime needed to paint it weighed six tons. It is the largest of the eleven surviving White Horses in Britain and is an imitation of the White Horse of Uffington in Berkshire.

(1738) THE WHITE HORSE OF KILBURN.—This figure was formed in November, 1857, by Mr. Thomas Taylor, a native of the village of Kilburn, in the valley below. The land on which the horse stands is (or was) the property of Mr. Dresser, of Kilburn Hall. Length, 180 feet; height, 80 feet; quantity of land covered; 3 roods; and to make a fence round would enclose two acres. Six tons of lime were used to give his skin the requisite whiteness, and 33 men were at work upon him on the 4th of November, the day on which he was completed. This figure was merely cut out to gratify the whim of the projector, not to commemorate any remarkable event. The following references appeared in a contemporary:—The White Horse of Kilburn, near Thirsk, was formed to commemorate a legend of a horse trainer, who was said to have been borne down a precipice, along with his steed and killed.

Thomas Taylor and the Uffington Horse

This 1902 card interestingly provides a description of the horse, as well as the usual picture. Thomas Taylor, a native of Kilburn and rich from his Yorkshire hams business in London, saw the Uffington horse and determined that Kilburn should have one of its own. It is visible forty miles away and was 'stabled' or covered over in World War II so as not to provide a landmark for German aircraft.

Kilburn, near Coxwold, Yorks.

Robert Thompson

The 16th century building in the old picture was Robert Thompson's home and design studio. Thompson's wood of choice was oak and he used an adze rather than a plane – a tool which created a wavy surface and emphasised the grain to beautiful effect – both characteristics of Thompson's work; his chosen style was classic 17th century English. The famous mouse signature came about, apparently, when he heard one of his carvers, Charlie Barker, say "We all as poor as church mice" whereupon Robert spontaneously carved a mouse on the church screen he was working on; he took it up as a symbol of industry in quiet places, and as his trademark. The new photo shows Kilburn today.

Easingwold Scouts' Camp, Kilburn August 1911

Easingwold Scouts' First Camp

Easingwold Scouts' first camp was held at Whit weekend in 1911 at Kilburn. Mothers were assured that the camp will be "healthy, instructive, and enjoyable," while the catering is "entirely in the hands of Mr Broad." To celebrate the troop's centenary the camp was 're-enacted' in 2011. The Easingwold Advertiser reports that a sketch was performed based on the first camp with the White Horse providing a prominent backdrop. The troop's website informs us that other activities included bridge-building, an assault course, shelter-construction, target-shooting for air rifles, instruction in bugle signalling and a demonstration of how Easingwold's Edwardian Scouts would have drummed on parade.

In 1910 the Advertiser reported that catering was for twenty-five boys; a century later there were more than 100 mouths to feed.

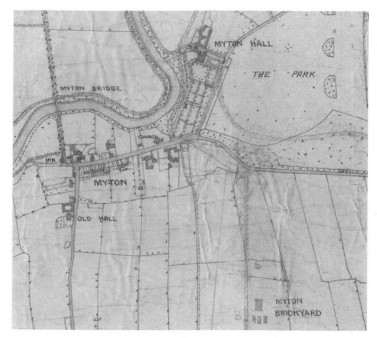

Myton on Swale Town Map 1868

Myton on Swale

Myton, on the confluence of the Swale and Ure (thus forming the River Ouse), is famous for three things: the White Battle or Battle of Myton Meadows in 1319, Myton Bridge, built in 1868 and Sir Miles Stapylton, one of the original Knights of the Garter. The older map of 1868 clearly shows the village layout before substantial changes took place. The Brickworks and the three worker's cottages - all long since demolished – are clearly visible as is the roadway leading to the river where bricks were loaded onto barges. Myton bricks were used to build York railway station and in the modernisation of the estate. The map also shows the location of the The Stapylton Arms, demolished by the Lord of the Manor in about 1910 following a drunken evening involving his staff. The 1933 Street Map is extracted from the original sale map of the village and effectively shows the village after the restoration and should be viewed in conjunction with the 1868 drawing. The numerals in bold refer to the plot numbers listed in the sale schedule.

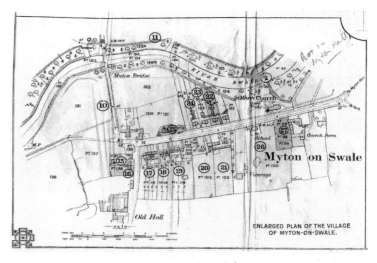

Myton on Swale Township map 1933

The Saracen's Head

Taken about 1910, Miles Stapylton is steering the horse drawn lawn mower in the older picture. In the fourteenth century his ancestor killed a Saracen chief in front of the Kings of England and France, and took the Saracen's head for a crest. You can still see this on some of the houses in the village (see page 120). Peter Bousfield points out that the hall itself is said to be modelled on a French chateau: 'Take a look at the picture...and then at the grass cutting photo: there are too many similarities to be just a coincidence, even down to there being a haha in front of the hall and the shape of the lawned entrance'. Myton Hall, then, would appear to be based upon the Chateau de la Morande (below), the family home of Victoria Aurellie. In 1868 Myton Hall and estate underwent a period of updating, the farms being based upon those on the Sandringham estate.

The White Battle

Various ladies outside Myton Hall and the Hall in 2012. In 1319 over 10,000 battle-hardened Scots under the Earl of Moray were heading for York, devastating everything in their path. They were finally confronted by a motley, untrained force of 10 -20,000 clerics and villagers under the Archbishop of York who were outflanked and massacred or drowned in the rivers. Over 4,000 died – many were ecclesiastics dressed in white robes, and so the conflict became known as the "White Battle". Writing in his 1891 Proelia Eboracensia (Battles Fought in Yorkshire) Alex Leadman was very definite about the lasting international consequences 'one of those sanguinary engagements with the Scotch which blot the pages of our earlier history, and which helped to render any union of the two countries an impossibility for several centuries'.

IN LOVING MEMORY OF
CAPTAIN MARTIN FREDERICK STAPYLTON R.N.
2ND SON OF MARTIN BRYAN STAPYLTON
2ND SON OF STAPYLTON STAPYLTON OF MYTON
BORN 1ST OCT: 1873
DIED 14TH NOV: 1932
"THERE'S A WONDROUS GOLDEN HARBOUR, FAR BEYOND THE SETTING SUN
WHERE A GALLANT SHIP MAY ANCHOR WHEN HER FIGHTING DAYS ARE DONE
FREE FROM TEMPEST ROCK AND BATTLE. TOIL AND TUMULT SAFELY O'ER
WHERE THE BREEZES MURMUR SOFTLY AND THERE'S PEACE FOR EVERMORE"
THIS TABLET IS ERECTED BY HIS WIDOW AND DAUGHTER

Jessie Gibson 1905

The English commanders at the battle were Sir William Meton, Archbishop of York; Sir John Hotham, Bishop of Ely and Chancellor of England; Nicholas Fleming, Mayor of York. Jessie Gibson was one of the eleven children of Thomas and Margaret Gibson. The older photograph was taken in the front garden of the then Post Office, which is now the White House in Myton. The Gibson family were joiners and undertakers in Myton for many years. The new picture shows the memorial tablet for Captain Martin Frederick Stapylton RN in St Mary's church. His wife was Ethel Horatia, nee Love; his daughter was Olive Love Stapylton.

Myton Bridge 1868

The old photograph shows the bridge, designed by Thomas Page – after working on Chelsea and then Westminster Bridge - just after work was completed on the flood bank around 1924. The new picture shows the fine bridge today with the Stapylton coat of arms. In 2003 it was refurbished using 20,000 specially made bricks made by the York Handmade Brick Company at Alne to replicate the intricate original Victorian brickwork. It is over 200ft long with a central span of 100ft made of three curved cast iron ribs 2ft 6ins deep. The original bridge contained about seventy tons of cast iron. Page was an assistant to Brunel and put forward one of the earliest plans for a Channel Tunnel.

The Apple Arch, Myton Hall

The Apple Arch, was an arch of apples which covered the Long Walk in the gardens. Residents of Myton Hall include Sir Kenneth Duncan Morrison CBE (b. 1931) Life President and former chairman of Wm Morrison Supermarkets plc. The firm was established in 1899 by William and Hilda Morrison as egg and butter merchants with market stalls in Bradford and Dewsbury. The new picture shows the walled garden, sadly somewhat derelict.

Myton for Sale, July 1933

A brass plaque above the entrance says the Hall was built in 1693 but a date in the 1680s seems more likely. Sir Brian Stapylton owned the Myton estate from 1679-1730. He engaged John Etty as architect. Not all the plots were sold off in the great 1933 sale, including the Hall; pencilled notes show details of price paid and the buyer on this page from the sale catalogue. The other photograph shows one of the Stapylton hatchments in the church – the black background on the left hand side indicates that the male is dead, while the female, indicated on the right, is still alive

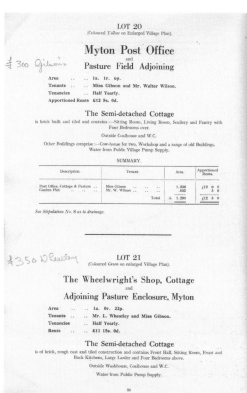

£300 Gibson

LOT 20
(Coloured *Yellow* on Enlarged Village Plan).

Myton Post Office
and
Pasture Field Adjoining

Area	..	..	1a. 1r. 6p.
Tenants	..	..	Miss Gibson and Mr. Walter Wilson.
Tenancies	..	Half Yearly.
Apportioned Rents £12 5s. 0d.

The Semi-detached Cottage
is brick built and tiled and contains :—Sitting Room, Living Room, Scullery and Pantry with Four Bedrooms over.

Outside Coalhouse and W.C.

Other Buildings comprise :—Cow-house for two, Workshop and a range of old Buildings. Water from Public Village Pump Supply.

SUMMARY.

Description.	Tenant.	Area.	Apportioned Rents.
Post Office, Cottage & Pasture ..	Miss Gibson	1.238	£12 0 0
Garden Plot	Mr. W. Wilson	.052	5 0
	Total	A. 1.290	£12 5 0

See Stipulation No. 8 as to drainage.

£350 W Pearley

LOT 21
(Coloured *Green* on enlarged Village Plan).

The Wheelwright's Shop, Cottage
and
Adjoining Pasture Enclosure, Myton

Area	..	..	1a. 0r. 22p.
Tenants	..	..	Mr. L. Wheatley and Miss Gibson.
Tenancies	..	Half Yearly.
Rents	..	..	£11 15s. 0d.

The Semi-detached Cottage
is of brick, rough cast and tiled construction and contains Front Hall, Sitting Room, Front and Back Kitchens, Large Larder and Four Bedrooms above.

Outside Washhouse, Coalhouse and W.C.

Water from Public Pump Supply.

24

FIDE. VIDE.

SED CUI

Pony and Trap

William and Anna Ward outside their home, Rose Cottage, taken about 1910. William was the Stud Groom at the estate and his wife Anna, the housekeeper. William it was who was responsible for planting the poplar trees in the village. During World War II Myton Hall was requisitioned as a convalescent and rehabilitation centre for the RAF. The saracen's head is one of a number to be seen on the facades of cottages in the village.

A Card to Gräfin (Countess) von Bismark

Peter Bousfield, owner of the card, explains: 'The 1913 postcard comes from the Estcourt family collection. Margaret Monica Stapylton, first cousin to Henry Miles Staylton married Mr G T J R Estcourt of Newnton House, Tetbury on 13 April 1863. There were previously strong connections between the Estcourts and the Stapyltons which continued for many years, both families having married into the European aristocracy. So receiving such a postcard would not have been unusual. In 1863 Henry Miles Stapylton married Victoria Aurellie, daughter of M. Gaston de Royer of the Chateaux de Morande, Sarthe, France'. What can be read of the card translates as follows: 'Thanks for your kind postcard from Basel. I am so pleased you had a comfortable stay here, and look forward to repeating your visit. I hope you returned safely to Lugano.' The Birkenau in question is the one in the Odenwald, Hessen, not the notorious Auschwitz-Birkenau.

Myton Leafy Pump

Taken around 1907 by JW Blackburn of Heckmondwicke. The original photograph appeared in The Beautiful and Historic Villages of Yorkshire (Illustrated), published in September 1907 by the proprietors of the Leeds and Yorkshire Mercury. It was made up of a number of photographs and articles of places around Yorkshire which were chosen by popular vote of the readers of the Leeds and Yorkshire Mercury.

The Stable Courtyard

Originally published in Down Your Way, Issue 67, June 2003 this speaks for itself. The new photograph shows the stables today, undergoing restoration

Malcolm Watson from Doncaster is thrilled with the information we have obtained on his mystery photograph first published in issue 64.

We can now confirm that it is, in fact, The Stable Courtyard at Myton Hall, Myton on Swale.

The Stapylton family owned the Myton estate from 1615 (although they had interests from 1599) along with other estates at Byland Abbey and Wass, near Coxwold, and Eston near Middlesbrough. Myton Hall was built in the 1630s and in 1690 was enlarged to its present size by Sir Bryan Stapylton.

The original stable doors are still there as is the water pump and apart from the fact the yard has been cobbled, very little has changed. The pump in the photograph bears the initials HMS and the date 1868. This stands for Henry Miles Stapylton who inherited the estate in 1864 from his father named, amazingly, Stapylton Stapylton. Together with his French wife they went to extraordinary lengths and considerable expense to improve the estate. New model farms were based on those built by the Prince of Wales (later Edward V11) at Sandringham and the architect who built Westminster Bridge was used to build the much smaller (!) Myton Bridge. The Major died in 1896 and having no issue left his estates to his nephew Lieutenant-Colonel Miles Stapylton. Miles Stapylton, his wife Norah and their four children would have been living at the hall when the picture was taken around the mid 1920s. The identity of the "staff" posing for this photograph remains a mystery but the man on the left is possibly a footman, the one next to him a coachman and the third (wearing motorcycling/driving apparel) is possibly a stable lad/groom or under gardener. The next one is, without doubt, a chauffeur wearing the typical attire of leather coat and gaiters.

Lieutenant-Colonel Stapylton was the last of the male line and died in 1931. Much of the estate was then broken up although his widow continued to live at the hall until it was used as a convalescent hospital for wounded service men in World War II. The hall (and the remainder of the estate) was finally sold in 1946 and is still a private residence.

George Weighell, Carter from Raskelf

The village has two particularly fascinating features: the first is the twelfth century St Mary's fifteenth century timber tower – one of only two in England, the other being St Andrew's at Greenstead-juxta-Ongar. Captain Augustus Frederick Cavendish Webb of the 17th Lancers is commemorated in the north chapel: he died of wounds sustained at the Charge of the Light Brigade at Balaclava in 1854. The second special feature is the Old Pinfold, or pound; pinfolds were built to hold animals which had strayed from their owner's land or were found grazing on common land without common rights. They were released after a fine or mulct had been paid to the pinder; breaking into a pinfold to release animals was punishable by a fine or imprisonment.

Sheriff Hutton

Everyone knows that Sheriff Hutton has a castle – what is less well known is that it has in fact had two castles: the earlier comprises a Norman motte and bailey structure from 1140 but only the mounds survive. This was built by Ansketil de Bulmer on land given to him by William the Conqueror for his support in the conquest. The Sheriff part of the village's name derives from its connections with the Bulmer family, Ansketil and Bertram de Bulmer being High Sheriffs of Yorkshire in 1115-1128 and 1128-1130 respectively. "Few villages touch national history so closely as Sheriff Hutton" So said John Rushton in his Ryedale Story. The village passed into the hands of the Neville family in 1115 and in 1382 John Neville began construction of the second castle which was completed in 1398. In 1484, Richard, Duke of Gloucester, set up the Council of the North, with its headquarters at Sheriff Hutton. After about 150 years the Council relocated to York and so began its gradual decline to the dramatic and imposing ruin we see today.

Sutton and Sterne

Laurence Sterne was vicar here (1713-68) but moved on to Coxwold when his parsonage burnt down. During his stay he published the first two books of Life and Opinions of Tristram Shandy, Gentleman, possibly basing it on the village and its characters. The novel was published over ten years from 1759-1769. A fine example of early Georgian architecture, Sutton Park was built by Thomas Atkinson. Apart from his own impressive house at 20 St Saviourgate in York Atkinson was responsible for remodelling the facade and gatehouse of Bishopthorpe Palace in the 1760s and for the chapel and facade of the Bar Convent in York. Sutton Park is noted for its Rococo plasterwork by Cortese, its collection of eighteenth century furniture and for its paintings, many of which came from Buckingham Palace.

Tollerton Ladies Cricket Club

Tollerton vs Tholthorpe 8th June 1909. Tollerton won. The name Tollerton derives from the village's position at one of the toll entrances to the Forest of Galtres where, according to Verstegan, travellers were given an armed guide to escort them on their journey to Bootham Bar, York. Gill, in his Vallis Eboracensis, adds 'it [the forest] was the lurking place of large hordes of banditti, who dwelt in caves and lived upon rapine and plunder'. In the seventeenth century the village was famous for horse racing on land close to the Great North Road. Drunken Barnaby, a celebrated road writer, tells us:

"Thence to Towlerton, where those stagers,
Or horses courses run for wagers;
Near to the highway the course is,
Where they ride and run their horses."

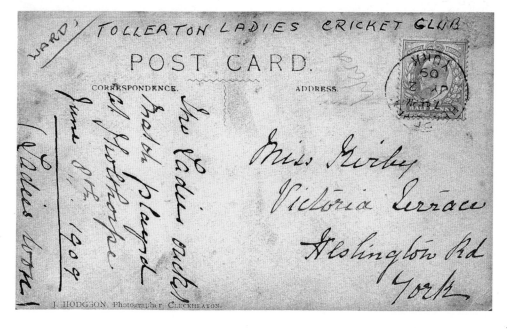

Wass

Wass used to be called Byland with Wass. Until 1924 it was an estate village owned first by the Stapyltons of Myton and then by the Wombwell family who sold it off. The Stapyltons were both grave-robbing absentee landlords, in the guise of Martin Stapylton or, with Major Henry Miles Stapylton, 'one of the best landlordes in England'. In his search for the grave of Roger de Mowbray Martin dug up what were thought to be his remains and reinterred them in Myton, taking with him sundry booty such as the High Altar slab, five chalices and tons of stone from the ruined abbey. Henry, however, sought to make amends for his grandfather's behaviour by reburying de Mowbray at Byland, giving the slab and chalices to Ampleforth and doing much needed repair work on the abbey. Furthermore, he paid for a village school in Wass in 1847, built Melrose Cottage for the schoolmaster and Yew Tree Cottage for the post office and postmaster.

The Wombwell Arms

The Wombwell Arms was built around 1620, not as a pub but as a granary using stone from nearby Byland Abbey which had become derelict. It became an ale house in about 1645 and was originally called The Stapylton Arms; the name was changed to The Wombwell Arms in 1896 when the village was bought by Sir George Wombwell of Newburgh Priory. In 1924 the village, including The Wombwell Arms, was sold off at auction. Russells of Malton bought the pub and then, Camerons of Hartlepool. In 1987 it reverted to being a free house. The middle picture on page 128 provides a mad dogs and Englishman type scene in the village while the lower photograph shows the dimunitive St Thomas Church.

New Row

Henry Miles Stapylton's schoolroom was put to use as a church on Sundays from 1866, and as a library and meeting room for 'Wass Mental Improvement Society', a variation on the Mechanic's Institutes. His philanthropy extended to the construction of a six model cottage terrace for his estate workers, 'New Row'. They were well ahead of their time with running water, kitchen ranges, and fireplaces in the bedrooms as well as in the living rooms. The yards boasted a coalhouse, pigsty, ashpit and privy; the families also had an allotment for growing vegetables. In 1896, Sir George Wombwell bought the estate; Wass remained an estate village until 17th September, 1924, when it was all sold off at auction in The Royal Station Hotel, York.

Husthwaite and William Peckitt

William Peckitt was born here in 1731 – one of England's foremost glass painters and stain glass makers – in fact he is widely regarded as the most prominent and prolific glazier of his day and responsible for keeping the craft alive in the 18th century. The family moved to York around 1750 where William worked in his father's glove making business before setting himself up as a glass painter in Colliergate. He died in 1795 and is buried in St Martin-cum-Gregory where Mary, his wife, made a memorial window to him in the church next to a memorial to two of his daughters by Peckitt himself.

WILLIAM PECKITT
(1731 - 1795)
Born in this village,
William Peckitt played a
major part in reviving the art
of stained glass painting
in this country.

The Black Bull, Husthwaite

Apart from extensive work on York Minster's famous glass and windows (notably the central sunburst motif to the Rose Window) Peckitt was also responsible for such glories as Burton Agnes Hall Window of Roger de Somerville; heraldic work at St Michael's Coxwold; Ripley Castle; Trinity College Cambridge library Alma Mater window; Lincoln Cathedral and windows at Oxford's Oriel College and New College. Above is Tom Conning with his horse outside the Black Bull in 1917 with his son and grandson. The name, Husthwaite, meaning house in the clearing, suggests a Danish origin; Domesday tells us in the entry for Bachesbi, that the township is described as having eight carucates of cultivated land. St Nicholas' Church is 12th century.